Self-Portrait with Tree

Poems

Rod Kessler

WINTER ISLAND PRESS
SALEM, MASSACHUSETTS

Self-Portrait with Tree: Poems
Copyright © 2024 by Rod Kessler

Winter Island Press

Published by Winter Island Press
Salem, Massachusetts
winterislandpress.com
ISBN: 979-8-9878655-4-5

In memory of Dudley H. Manchester, my English teacher at Hartford High, and of the spoken arts poetry collection on vinyl in the main branch of the Hartford Public Library.

ACKNOWLEDGMENTS

Anima
"Late delivery"

Arete
"Fission"

Balcones
"Flight"

A Break in the Clouds
"*El Señor Profesor*"

Calliope
"Self-Portrait with Tree" and "On the Edge of It"

Chariton Review
"The Elm Tree on Lafayette Street"

Interim
"Fall Term, the Course Begins" and "January Thaw"

The Leaflet- NEATE
"Another Immaculate Conception"

The Lowell Pearl
"Memorial"

New Mexico Humanities Review
"Somewhere South of Miami"

Odessa Poetry Review
"Cold Comfort, February 1985"

Off the Coast
"Word Problem"

The Pink Chameleon
"Final Exam" and "Pathetic Fallacy"

Ploughshares
"Apartheid"

Poetry Soup Magazine
"Unsmiling [on Mass Ave]" and "Campus
Wisdom at Commencement"

Soapbox
"Rigor Mortis"

CONTENTS

PREFACE

Most Americans dislike poetry because of how it's taught in the lower grades— or at least how it was taught when I was a kid. A poem was a kind of scary intelligence test. At best, a puzzle. What is Emily Dickinson saying in "'Hope' is the thing with feathers"? Or What symbolism is Robert Frost employing in "The Road Not Taken"? I'm still baffled by Dickinson, but I was lucky in my teachers, the handful who could hear the mermaids singing, and I found my way to Shelley and Whitman, Masters and Sandberg, Pound and Wilbur, Plath and Sexton, Sharon Olds and Philip Levine, and so on.

Naturally enough I wrote poems, not many, but maybe enough. I thought of myself not as a poet but as a friend of poetry and of poets. My calling would be fiction writing. At Salem State, I was expected to teach fiction writing, of course, but not only that. There was poetry writing and nonfiction too (yes, and lots and lots of freshman comp). So, over my three decades there I wrote poetry along with my students, often shaping work to illustrate the issues of craft we discussed in class.

I also wrote a novel, a long one topping over 600 pages in manuscript. (Whatever its merits, commercial appeal evidently was not one of them, and Edelman Unsung remains unpublished.) Among the book's characters is a poet—a mercurial, sometimes strident, sometimes witty, feminist poet. Her poems are a feature of this novel. I wrote them.

This collection of poems is a mix: the poems I've
written for myself all along, the poems written
with the didactic issues of craft in mind, the
poems of my imagined feminist firebrand.
Perhaps you can tell which is which.

It's been said that when poets turn to fiction
writing, the results are often beautiful, with a
prose surface that simply sings and with
observations that are as subtle as they are precise.
And yet, and yet, when we fiction writers turn to
writing poetry . . . well, often it's best to just avert
your eyes.

May it not be the case here.

Self-Portrait with tree

FINAL EXAM

1.   I come to your apartment
for my clothes. You feel:
__a) Abandoned
__b) Relieved.

2.   I lug away cartons
heavy with books,
shoes. I find your arms
around me:
__a) You still love me
__b) You feel sorry for me
__c) Old habits.

3.   You lie in bed at night,
the shades drawn,
the clock gleaming
its blue digits:
__a) You turn your back
      to the empty spot
      where I belong
__b) You stretch
      like a spring uncoiling
__c) You're asleep

4.   In your dreams:
 __a) You speak a language
      I can't hear
__b) I slip from you like an anchor
__c) You meet a stranger

ON THE EDGE OF IT

It is early now, not even six,
and sleep is something that happens
to somebody else, to people we don't know.
The street starts to fill with traffic.
Each car and truck strikes like a match, flaring
across an asphalt matchbox, burning away
into silence. I am watching. The arc-lamp
streetlight is orange. Twenty miles off
in another town you lie, unsleeping, eyeing
a digital clock. The blue numbers
knock the minutes off with the glazed
indifference of a gas meter.
You count the worries of your life—
the job, the kid, the rent-control board,
the empty, other half of the bed
I still think of as ours.
You sit on the edge in darkness.
If either of us were a smoker,
now would be the time for it. We hold
nothing in our fists but our fingers.
You're switching on your light now.
I, mine. We're switching on lights
in two countries. From a spy-plane
or a hot-air balloon, someone
could take us both in, could fit us
into the same frame one more time.

From above, the earth seems to be burning,
not in flames but in embers. Morning
birds are screaming. The land between us
stretches out, glowing, like a bed of coals.

SOMEWHERE SOUTH OF MIAMI

Somewhere not exactly on the map,
we came to a splintering pier
on spider-leg piles at the end
of a hard day's drive
from yesterday's hard day's drive.
Over the water the horizon line
opened its mouth for the hot orange pill.
There was beer. Daylight went and
the turquoise sea soured.
Soon a rising tide nipped our toes.
We had a flashlight.
I played the beam on the curdling waters.
Something taut and nebulous stirred
and turned below the flimsy boards.
Eyes set as far apart as mine
caught in the light. How red those eyes were.
They glowed like brake lights on a Pontiac.
If this was a shark, it had a neon brain.
I yanked my legs up and off we ran,
fifteen hundred miles or so
northward, and we're still running.
So much for creatures on the edge.

FROZEN PLANET

I was a frozen planet
lost in space, drifting
through regions dark and cold.
What atmosphere I'd had
was blown away by cosmic winds.
My waters? Locked in frozen vaults
where no one would find them
or think to look.
Time stalled, waiting for eternity.
Then you, warm star, swept me
into orbit. Around your core
I spun. And look at me now—
rivers splashing down mountainsides,
birds calling in the treetops,
apes ranging in the savannahs,
monkeys squawking in the canopies.

FOR WHAT'S-HER-NAME

You are like something.
Is it the scent
the meadow spent
in the breeze?
The browned mountains
of evening
humped like camels
sleeping in the trees?
No, that's not right,
not you.
Nor is it true
that you are like
the ivory chill
of a Moslem moon.
Who are you?
Did you steal
beyond my capacity
to respond
in simile?
I could say more
you fox--
you even slip
the locks
of metaphor,
And then like birds
you fly away
without words.

FALL TERM, THE COURSE BEGINS

Anew. I stalk the classroom like some
tree shrew dispossessed. The shade spins
up its roller with a slap. Welcome
to EN203, I say: Writing Verse.
You drag your hapless chairs in a ring
about my desk. This is worse
than kindergarten, you think. You speak
of poems somehow as though you'd set
your student bodies anywhere to get
three easy credits. At least there's a view
out the window: rooftops, green hills,
the day's accumulation of clouds. A few
gaunt pigeons huddle to the sills
and listen, their hidden feet
unmetrical if free. I'm perching too
atop the wooden desk. The worksheet
in my hand will interest some of you
as much as tears interest sleeping dogs.
I see the clock on the wall
where your dozing gazes fall.
But even time is moved by measured cogs.

LIKE ME (A colloquy)
for Tony Hoagland

Of the silence within when you hold me
a person like me thinks,
Feelings are for the young,
the friction of moving parts that time
in time with make smooth.

Of the way I have no answer
when you say you love me, a person
like me thinks, *A heart so dried*
is a raisin of no sweetness, a tough jewel
you can never melt on your tongue.

Of the way I fall asleep while you
lie there, your questions lingering,
a person like me thinks,
Love is a timebomb
in reverse, an explosion
followed by a ticking, ticking,
ticking ending in silence.

WINSOME? LOSE SOME (song)

However fine his bright bouquets
at night the florist throws away
each beauty mottled with decay,
each rose that's mottled with decay.

If placid geese will mate for life
consider the unceasing strife
the gander knows who lacks a wife,
the solo flyer sans a wife.

Some stars are lights that no one sees.
And hidden forests hide great trees
In me compassions seem to freeze.
I cannot satisfy, amuse, or please.

NINTH INNING STRETCH

And as for whether we have that much
in common anymore, say what you mean
to say. If you think I'm such
a stranger, why do you lean
so hard on me that you fatigue
us both? Listen, the danger always lay
apart from us, away, in league
with wood owls, rats, and things that day-
light shields us from—wolf wail, fox bark,
bat shrill. Yet you call me alien
now, "stranger," part of the dark
well you're pooling free from. When
will you get it right?
You've lived in me, daughter? son?
Kin, twin, double-one.
When will you see the light?

POET AT HOME

Robert Hass is doing haiku
on Channel 2 when the telephone rings.
The caller wants "a few minutes only."
He says *survey, consumer, product information.*

"I'm in middle of something," I break in.
"Red Sox game," I tell him." Call tomorrow."

Then I'm the poet's again. We do
a six-line poem. Safe at home.

II
Robert Hass is reading haiku on Channel 2.
The ringing phone rings again, rings, goes quiet.
Fish might see bait and not bite hook.

III
Husband at desk struggling with poem.
Wife talking about bills to couples' therapist.

FLIGHT

The season is winter.
The landscape, desert.
The horizon is as blank
as a women's silence.
What pushes me onward
is not hope
but the refusal to hope.
I have kept at it for eight weeks,
now nine. In the compass I keep
the one red arrow pierces me
near where I breathe and will
not budge. The people I meet
are mirages, whispering
about water, grasses, loam.
When they reach out to me
they turn into nothing.
The air is sharp with absence,
sliced with your shadow.
You loom behind me like the Sierras.
I think that if I turn
I could still touch you.
Like everything else, distance
deceives me. The coyotes
are laughing. They see
that I've come nowhere,
that I make no progress
to speak of. I must keep
going, I am so lost.

REACHING AN OASIS IN THE SEXUAL DESERT

At last I've lain again all night
in someone's arms. Come morning
you say how happy I've made you,
saying it again and again. I panic,

flee to the streets of a strange
(but dimly familiar) city.
I'm steering into a cul-de-sac so steep
and narrow I can't turn around.

Now in the laundromat the mess
of yesterday's T-shirt and boxers floats
in the foaming cycle. A pocket mouse
hops in view, cheek pouches bulging

with cactus seed, its tiny hands held up
to reassure me, saying,
At least we can carry on now,
another six months without water.

PATHETIC FALLACY

On a whim of her own
my therapist phones you.
This is a private matter—
No billing. He isn't
your mother, she tells you.
This is no time to leave him.
But even in fantasy
who is whose mother?
Everyone sees this but me.
And you are as relentless
in wrecking me
as the incoming waves
I drive past each morning
heading for campus.
In front of my students
I give away nothing.
My tie is as right
as a promise. But when
I tell about the bomb
sinking through the sky
onto Hiroshima,
they come away thinking
I'd been there.

MATH PROBLEM

A man walked down the dirt road
into the deep woods, walking three dogs.
Half an hour later, he returned
with only two. Is there a problem?

APARTHEID

My students, pink as Barbie dolls,
clean as the coins they slip
into arcade games at the mall,
live in tenements of ignorance.
Headlines are meant for someone
else's worry, like taxes
or insurance on the Camarro
which Dad sees to.
When it comes to Winnies,
they don't know Mandela
from Pooh. In the film we watch
black women march against
the pass law. For all but one
month of the year, they must
live apart from their husbands.
In tribal homelands
children go hungry. Black
flies move across their faces
like hopeless pilgrims. In a city
the cops drop clubs across
the backs of black men carrying
placards. The drinking fountain
is marked Europeans Only.
The police raise their rifles
and the fleeing blacks leave shoes
behind, cheap waffled plastic.

The light comes on.
You turn your faces to me.
As ever you say nothing.
My questions die in the air.
The clock tells you to file out.
Later in your journals you
write about injustice.
The wives should get
to be with their husbands
all year. It must be so lonely,
like not being allowed to date.

CAMPUS WISDOM AT COMMENCEMENT

The brick wall argues persistence.
The unclouded sky counsels a light touch.
The pathway urges direction, "Go forth!"
The scented yellow bush favors roots.

What's left of the squirrel pressed onto the road
promises that our sufferings will end.
And the silence that slips around our noises—
what says the silence if not *lies, lies, lies?*

FISSION

In a screening room as grey
as history, my students slump
in their seats like bags of groceries
waiting to be lifted into somebody's
station wagon. The Bomb, hanging
from a parachute, sinks on Hiroshima
like an anchor. We feel the flash.
A chair leg groans across the floor.
Beneath its black helmet the brow
of Japan boils. In close-ups
people are charred like badly broiled
chickens, skins peeling off bodies
like rinds. Nobody coughs. Truman's face
fills the screen now and there's a parade
in New York City. Houselights come on.
Twenty freshmen shift their eyes to me
with the gratitude of netted salmon.
Their essays come in later, ripped
like challenges from spiral notebooks,
the edges jagged.

WORD PROBLEM

Jillian has been depressed twelve of the last twenty-eight days. On four days, she was unsure how she felt. On nine days so furious was she that Carl fled Tucson toward Taos, a distance of six-hundred miles. If he travels sixty miles an hour, the legal limit, and she follows three hours later, traveling at eighty, how far will Carl go before he drives Jillian crazy?

Will it take longer or shorter if she refuses her green capsule?

Hint: In the desert, distances loom vaster than they appear.

SELF-PORTRAIT WITH TREE

The sycamore just off
from the center of things
in Sunderland, with its canopy broad enough
to take in all of Route 47 and a swath
of lawn, hedge, and sidewalk--
It would take three of me,
hand to hand and hand to hand again
to engirdle that trunk. How I'd like that,
and so would I,
and so would I.

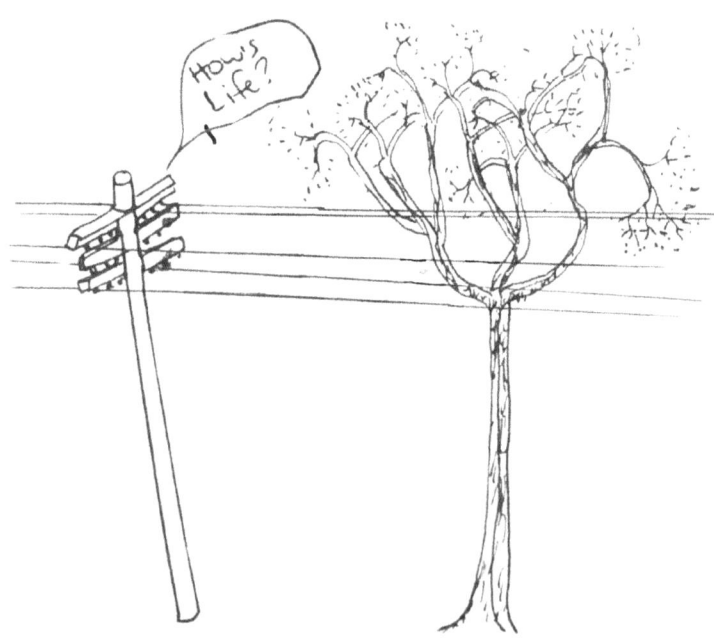

JANUARY THAW

-North Hadley, Mass.

The hard foot of winter
unballs its toes
and this moist clay
stinks with the hope
of next spring's roots.
Tomorrow the river
grows its skin of ice
finger thin. Then fist
thick, then boot thick
and brutal. Hard winter
wears its boots again,
and moves slow,
marching through
to the end of April,
the sweet heifers
shaking in their stalls.

COLD COMFORT, FEBRUARY 1985

My window is the itch
the winter branches
on a windless day
long to scratch. Such
trees only look dead,
you'd say. You'd hate it
here, feel hemmed in,
claustrophobic among
maples and elms.
You like vistas, things
at a distance. One time
when we were still near-
strangers, I drove you
to the desert near Sasabe.
You had been sad
(Why, you didn't say).
We stopped in the middle
of nowhere, got out,
leaned against the car.
Chollas barbed the roadside,
scatterings of ocotillo.
You gazed at mountains
as far away as possible.
Everything made you happy.
A year later I took you
East, to birch trees,

granite, snow. The nearness
of things oppressed you.
You pined here, hemlocked.
Pressed to the window you made
a hammer of your hand. The glass
fissured. With a shard you wrote
hieroglyphics in your arm.
What you wrote there
was your ticket home.
Another year has passed
and I too am sad. At my window
I see beyond the trees
to the trees beyond. I watch so still
I see the gaunt sticks grow.
I've been going nowhere
fast, why not try slow?

WHITE FLAG IN VERMONT

Those swaying firs that rise above
the roofline are hurling down
their snow bombs. Hear them thud.
What rumors of air, what stirrings of spirit
have set them off? The imam of wind?
The ayatollah of thaw? Caught out,
they make no run for it, they
can't. But unburdened of their cold
and heavy grievance, they raise
and wave enlightened branches,
raising and waving,
sighing with relief.

THE ELM TREE ON LAFAYETTE STREET

Thinks it's all junk these days, the routine,
insistent parade of Toyotas and Broncos
heading up to the college, the kid in the pick-up
getting out the freebie Sunday paper every Saturday
around ten, the ladies boarding the 455 bus, two quarters
and a dime in hand, handbags full of certainties.
The Latin guys without jobs spend their mornings
on benches across from the donut shop and the Catholic
Church. In the frame shop, the artist who could do better
work with her eyes closed takes her time mounting yet
another print of Monet's garden from the museum shop
in the city. At Major MagLeashe's, the proprietor
squinting at daylight shows the door to the smells
of yesterday's beer spills. This is all junk, thinks
the great elm on Lafayette Street. It was junk
forty years ago too, for that matter, when little boys
wore ties every Monday for assembly at the Middle School,
the girls blue dresses, even though they didn't want to,
and all the mommies stayed home and had private breakdowns
and cooked chicken a la king. It is junk
and was junk, thinks the elm, whose every heavy limb turns
upward in its own sweet, unrepeated & rococo way. Limbs?
Branches? Only in the most literal sense wooden,
thinks the elm. The tree thinks its trunk and branches
are a jazz statement, as though jazz could be something
other than sound. Well, why the hell not, this elm tree
thinks. Just look at me. And it bugs him that we don't get it.

HAIKU FOR MARCH

Under thunderclouds
these daffodils, that crocus
Is spring still coming?

DOING WITHOUT

Last Saturday I left a winter glove
somewhere. It was lumpy, numb, made of
thermal plastics—synthetic near-wool, tan
going grey. But it's been home for a hand
three Januaries now. I've kept its mate.
A boy in a book I had when I was eight,
a French boy, lost *le do de son clarinet.*
His *do* was gone, his scale began with *re.*
Here was a puzzle. Where would you have to go
to find his insubstantial *do?* Suppose
you had to find it. Would you drum the air?
I'd try it gloveless, raw-boned; fingers bare.

VILLAGE POETESS

The beautician at her station draws a comb
down the scalp of her customer, forehead to crown,
crown to nape, her pulling hand tensioned to a point
of efficiency that makes it all seem effortless.

She regards her customer's hair the way her father,
atop his green John Deere monster, regards
the neat fifteen furrows of alfalfa in the high field
above the road to Cambridge Junction, or the way
her mother, head teller in the Merchant branch
by the strip mall with the P.O. and the G.U. store
regards the day's accumulation of deposit slips.

Of the salon mirror she takes no notice: she's seen it
all before—Mrs. Larson's complacent slump
of resignation, her eyes closed, her thoughts god knows
where, perhaps on her boy gone off with the Guard
to Kandahar, or whether to fill the seat on the town
committee studying traffic calming devices
for the corner of Pearl and Main.

This late in the day, the slanted sunlight paints
the one white salon wall a warming glow. It's a job.

If she had her druthers, she'd take a load off
and sink into some upholstered chair someplace
else, in good lamplight, where, paper in hand,
she'd launch a poem of her own, something
of how expectations recede like ice
on the Gihon in early spring or like the line
of sunlight sinking on the wall at day's end.

She would write a long one with long lines
that you had to take your time with, both writing
and reading, lines like separate strands that
you could tease with your fingertips but that,
interwoven, took shape, and held.

She'd like that, a long time in a silent space,
with only herself to please, with no one saying,
"Emily, O Emily dear, short, cut it short!"

HOME EC

After she showed us hospital corners
and how to make the top sheet taut,
after she showed us the straight seam
and the hidden stitch and the gusset,
after we saw where the fork went
and the bread plate, after she had us
stand and walk and wait like a lady,
after we learned to knead and bake,
after we saw how to enter and greet
and take our seat, after she showed us how
to draw a man out and discover
whatever he loved and did well
and knew to never speak at length
about ourselves
or give a speech but
only to bring him
into the light and let him shine—
after she taught us this in that basement room
with its Frigidaires, its shiny stoves,
its fixtures of chrome, she went home
to three empty rooms and made evening
after evening out of sherry bottles and brandy.

PRIMER

The work of the teacher? Fitting the harness.
The work of the mother? Softening the blow.
The work of the lover? Weaving a net
of imaginary thread that holds and binds.
For the wise the work is healing with old lies.

So if your hand shakes, scatter seeds.
If your thoughts grow dark, lie fallow.
And if the taste in your mouth goes
as sour as the smell behind the wall
place your life between your teeth
and bite down hard.

ANOTHER IMMACULATE
CONCEPTION

Say it was near Christmas
an immaculate conception
as all our births must be.
(Wasn't yours?)
Or should we suppose
our moms and dads
did the humpty-dumpty dance for us?
It's inconceivable. The two
don't even talk.
But in nine months' time—
in less time than it takes
to wear out a tire—
I was a ripe peach on the bough,
hanging, as dependent as an ornament,
the red tomato,
the big enchilada.

LITTLE BOY

I fell to the people of Hiroshima
on a parachute, sullen, like a debutante
ballerina brooding, reluctant to pass
from the wings. The detonation,
more than a moment, lingered like a chord.
Can you deny the beauty of my display?
I made the sky boil with red blackness.
The city beneath me applauded
in a paroxysm of flame. They were dying
by the thousands to see me.
I made the Emperor weep.

THE DEAF BOY

The deaf boy's father can't understand him.
The child of three, maybe four, stares up at a man
my own age, on Arlington Street near the great
home church of the Unitarians and the newsstand
by the Green Line, hawking the *Globe*
and the *Herald*, and gum, sundries, and who-knows-
what-all else. From below comes the clatter of the trolleys,
and the traffic announces its noisy unimportance.
The boy hears none of this. Great, putty-colored plastic slugs
encircle his ears, and I can see the line of light
distorting in the thickness of his glasses.
His fists clenched, this little boy—he's blond,
for what it's worth, in short pants with knees
showing bony—, with tears on his face, is shouting
again, way up to his father. The man crouches to be
not so high, and it's not that he doesn't want to understand.
He's shaking his head while the boy tries again,
the chords moving roughly along his little throat.
From where I watch, it sounds like he wants a Marlboro.
Marlboro! Then I think he's saying Raleighs. Raleighs.
(What is it with me?) The father tries to hug the boy.
It isn't helping. That night they're with me
in my dreams. I am smoking, the dad is smoking,
the little guy, quiet now, is smoking.

LATE DELIVERY
to Freddy, 1952-1969,
on the anniversary of his death

In a dream I see you spooning
rubble through the chute
of the mailbox on our street.
God The Father, like Dad
with his eyes popping out,
catches you in the act.
He moves at you without a word
like a wrestler angling for a pin.
You don't see him. I shout,
stand between you, my arms out
stiff. In hospital green He's gowned
for surgery—not to save you
but to cut you out. He's fresh
from the reactor, from the isotope
machine. The package in his hand
is for His Boy, His little Son.
Stamped with iridescent triangles,
 it's radioactive "but safe," He claims.
"What fools you liberals are."
Then you stalk off, your face
vacant with the look they combed
on you in your coffin. Once more,
alone, I'm left to listen.
And Susan Monsky comes, who told me

not three weeks ago to drown
myself in a bathtub. Her shoulders
are too bony to cry on. And then,
like the shutter falling through
a camera, the delivery. I saw
not light but darkness. I wept,
crushing my eyes upon her wool
coat until I woke in blankets,
the sky blue, the piles of snow
disappearing. I got
the letter you sent me.

WOMEN IGNITE!

You witches, whores, shrews--
disgruntled with your life
in the tiresome role of wife?
Arise and light the fuse

As alien as loosestrife,
as swollen as a bruise?
Become your own midwife
and light the fuse

Cleave to loss, to change—
to what's new and strange.
Unring your finger and without ruse
ignite the fuse.

PROPHECY

A brutish man knoweth not
Neither doth a fool understand this
--psalms

Come not into this city seeking absolution
come not, like a pilgrim, to seek our healing balm.
We know what you did when the world was yours:
you plastered asphalt on our meadows, sunk
our land beneath so many K-Mart parking lots.
You filled our history books with John Wayne movies
and made a White House puppet from a box of 40-mule
team Borax. So the wells ran dry and the air went bad,
and the bread turned to cardboard, and milk
into chemical soup. Once the wheels stopped wheeling
and the roaring ceased, once the radios filled with roaches
and silverfish, we who had been invisible to you,
who saw to the dishes and sheets and daughters,
we shadows rose from the dungeons of obscurity
tired of the moral purity of our victimhood.

RIGOR MORTIS

For Raine Jones

The world is a bed of wet cement:
a trap for the comfortable and settled.

Move along, move on, I tell you.
Once the cake hardens around your feet

you'll need a jackhammer crew
to escape and few do. The world

is a plain of women in concrete
shoes, some caught reaching up

to clotheslines, some perched over
keyboards, some standing at blackboards,

index fingers pointing. Beware
of standing still. With the wrong luck

you could become a monument to yourself
and we know what birds do to statues.

UNSMILING [ON MASS AVE]

Watch: How it lies holstered in your qualms.
Better: This frown so effective with beggars.
Better still: The tight-mouth face that says nothing
and moves on. Yet we hunger for one another.
I mean you, stranger: You on this main street
vending its pleasantries: its ice cream, pastries,
custom frames. Can you see me: gray-bearded
and beagle-eyed? Note your surrounds:
The old become mere scenery. Like lamp posts
and mailboxes we appear only to disappear.
Can you believe that I once was you? Laugh.
Talk into your cell phone. Follow some advice:
Stay young! Stay young! Stay young!

EL SEÑOR PROFESOR

Señor Profesor, let no man call you old.
The age of seventy is a bend in the river
you have yet to navigate. When you were young
the poor of your country ate *frijoles negros*,
you, filet mignon. How well you recall
your family estate in Oriente province.
Here in our country you teach the young
the secrets of free enterprise,
how the circulating dollar is spent
to be re-spent, how a nation's debt is its wealth.
The house you bought beyond the lawns of our campus
is older than you are. The great tree in your yard
was a seed in the year of the birth of José Martí.
This evening, starlings flock to it by the thousand.
If you listen, you can understand them,
they too come from the south.
What is their torment? Are they hungry?
You've brought a rifle
and you come at them waving your arms.

SLEEP APNEA

It paces, waiting
to vault up to the crack
of light and air

atop your clotted
throat. With every leap
it jolts you

across your mattress,
your arm
thrashing.

When it quiets.
you hunker in your blanket
willing the dawn.

Listen. Listen.
It is still in you,
It wants out.

EATING THE DEAD

I was slow to learn the art
of eating the dead. At eight
I could barely keep my zeida Harry down.
Yet by twenty I was ready for my brother,
who lacked the heart to make it past sixteen.
My high school pal Dave Edgar lost his lungs at thirty
and went out as gray as the nuclear subs he serviced.
Martin, my college friend, struck out
at forty (The heart, the heart, the…)
Sweet Peggy, who'd giggled in braces
in junior high, was betrayed by breasts
that would never nurse a child.

My mother's father. My father's mother.
Now barely a year goes by without its bloody meal.
Ed Abbey wrote his final book yet left the world unchanged.
May Sarton faded off without a last goodbye. Small matter.
I eat the dead every day now, my dead, and I'm getting
heavy.

MEMORIAL

In dying, you've shrunk,
like a tire someone let the air
out of.
You lie in the wooden box
as dry as a kitchen match.
Those fingers would snap like twigs
if I dared unbend them.

On this most family
of Jewish moments, my stout uncle
cigar in hand
lurches at the sight of you
and says O Jesus.
Your three daughters,
decked out from Saks,
don't even try to look.
You ran a men's wear store
in Brooklyn, over the Bridge.
Choice, not chance, brought a man
to Maxis. We grandsons stand around
in fine black suits. My brother's vest
fits like a tee. Your tailors stand proud.
and I've left the silver stud
from my ear
on my dresser top back in Boston.

I raise my camera but the family wants
the lens cap on. I could take black pictures
of your death but you've turned white on us.
They screw down the lid
forever on you. Can anyone sing
Kaddish? God,
it's moments like these
that make me glad I'm immortal.

WINTER ISLAND PRESS
SALEM, MASSACHUSETTS

Winter Island Press edits and publishes books that reflect the breadth and bounty of human experience. Our roster of authors represents a vibrant tapestry of voices. We are delighted to work with both seasoned writers and promising debut authors who contribute to the literary mosaic that defines Winter Island Press. We value creativity, originality, and craftsmanship. From fun and potent fiction to thought-provoking non-fiction and poetry, Winter Island Press publications offer narratives that leave a lasting impact on readers' hearts and minds.

If you have a compelling manuscript that aligns with our vision, or even a great idea for one, we'd love to hear from you. Connect with us through our website, winterislandpress.com.